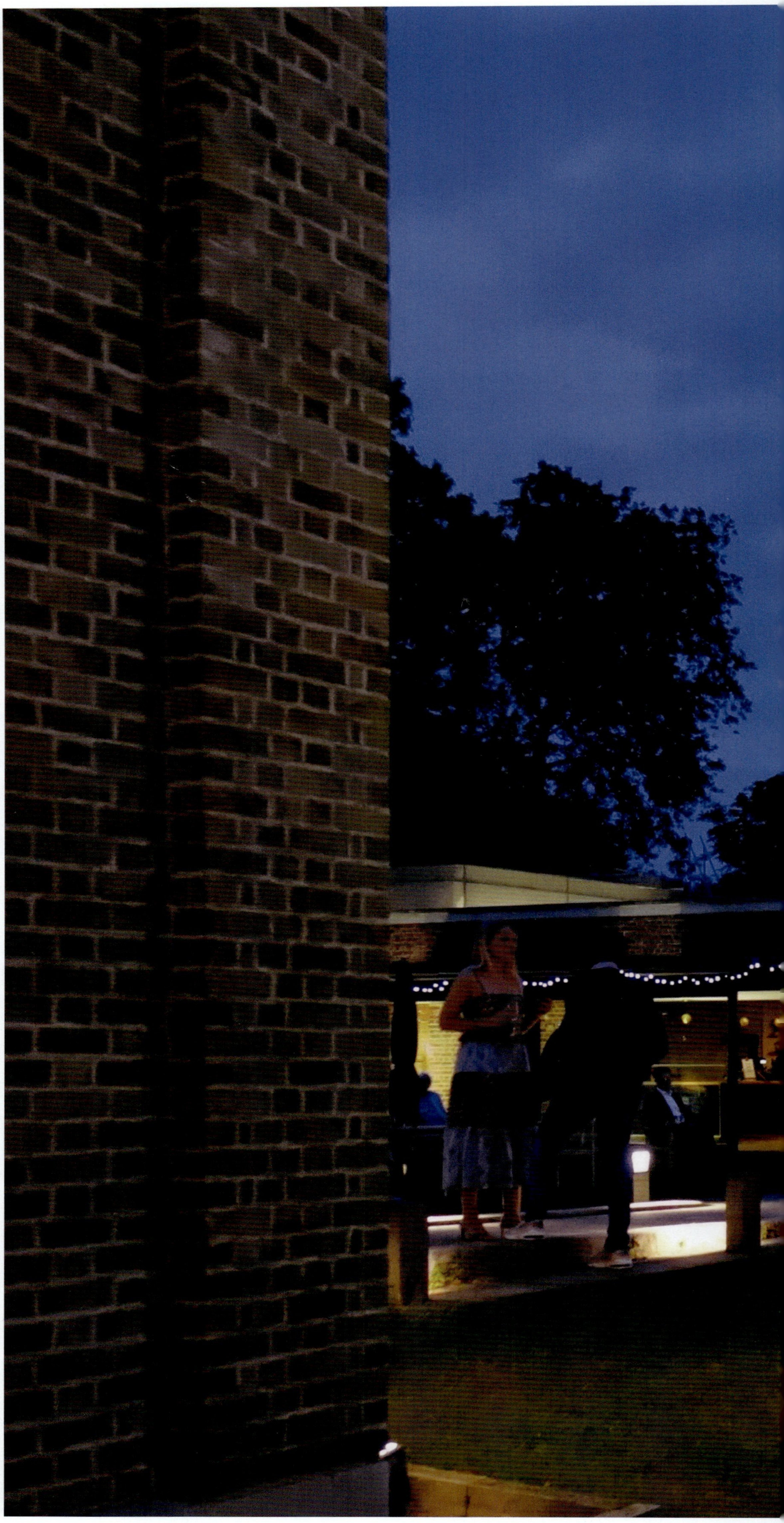

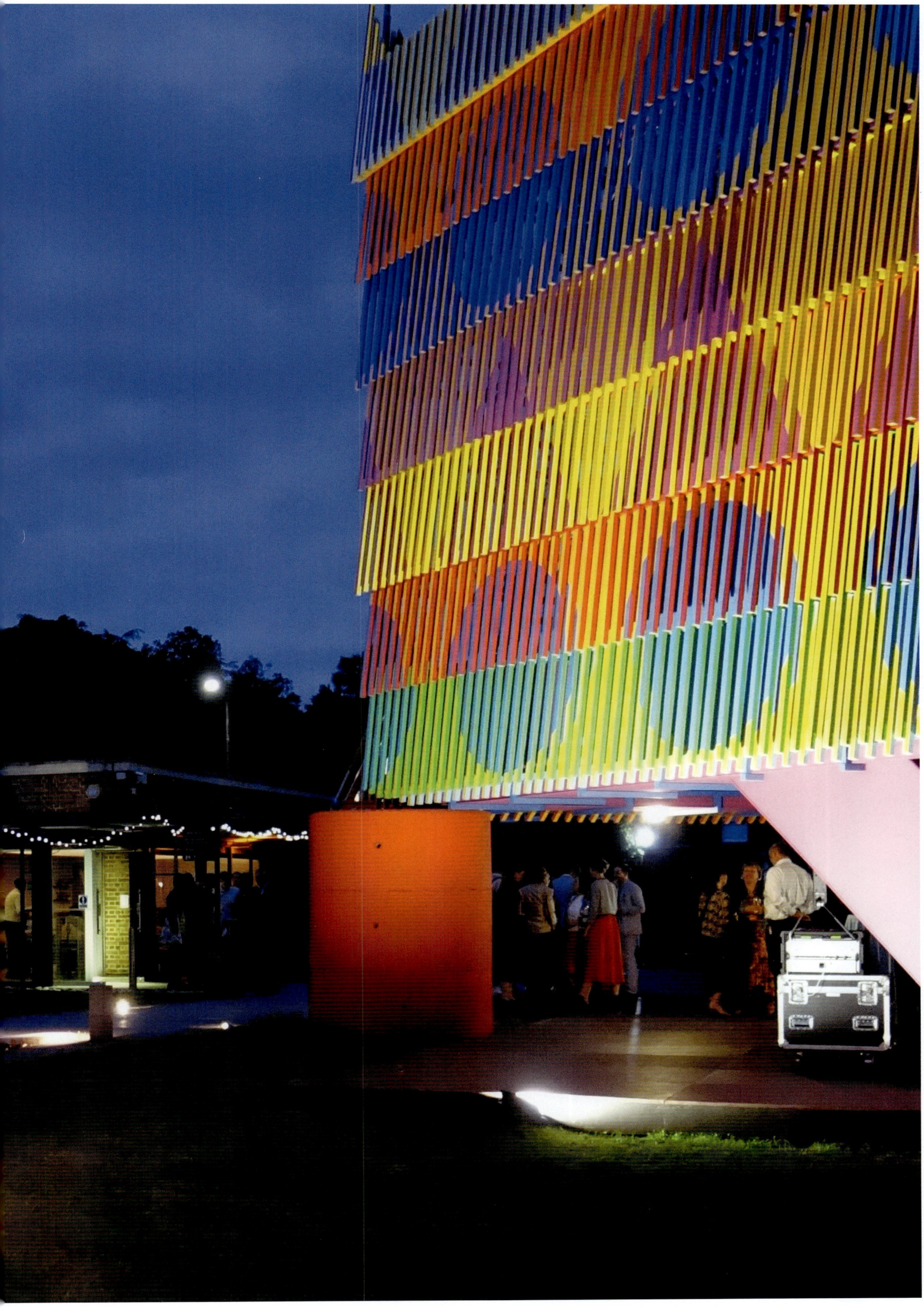

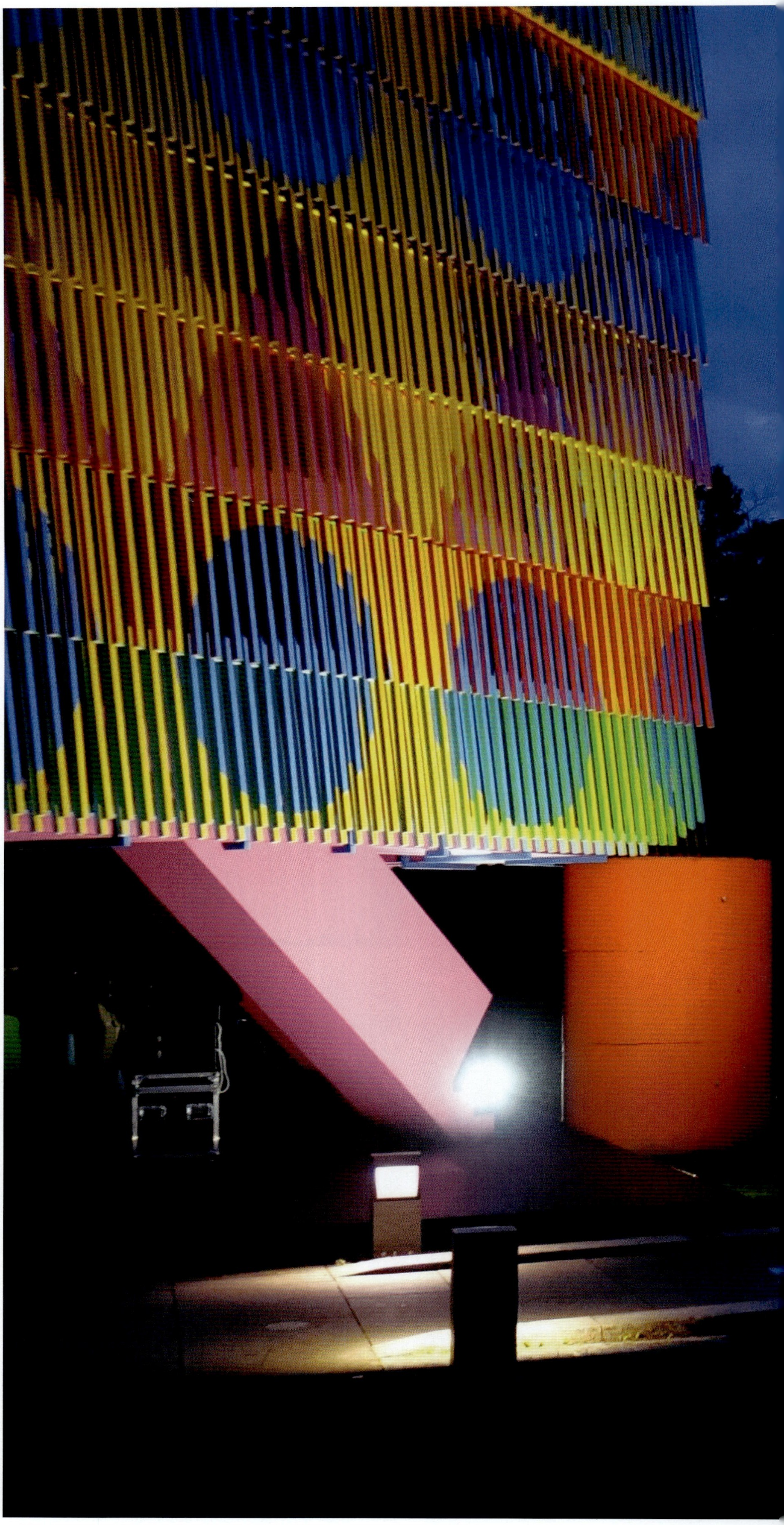

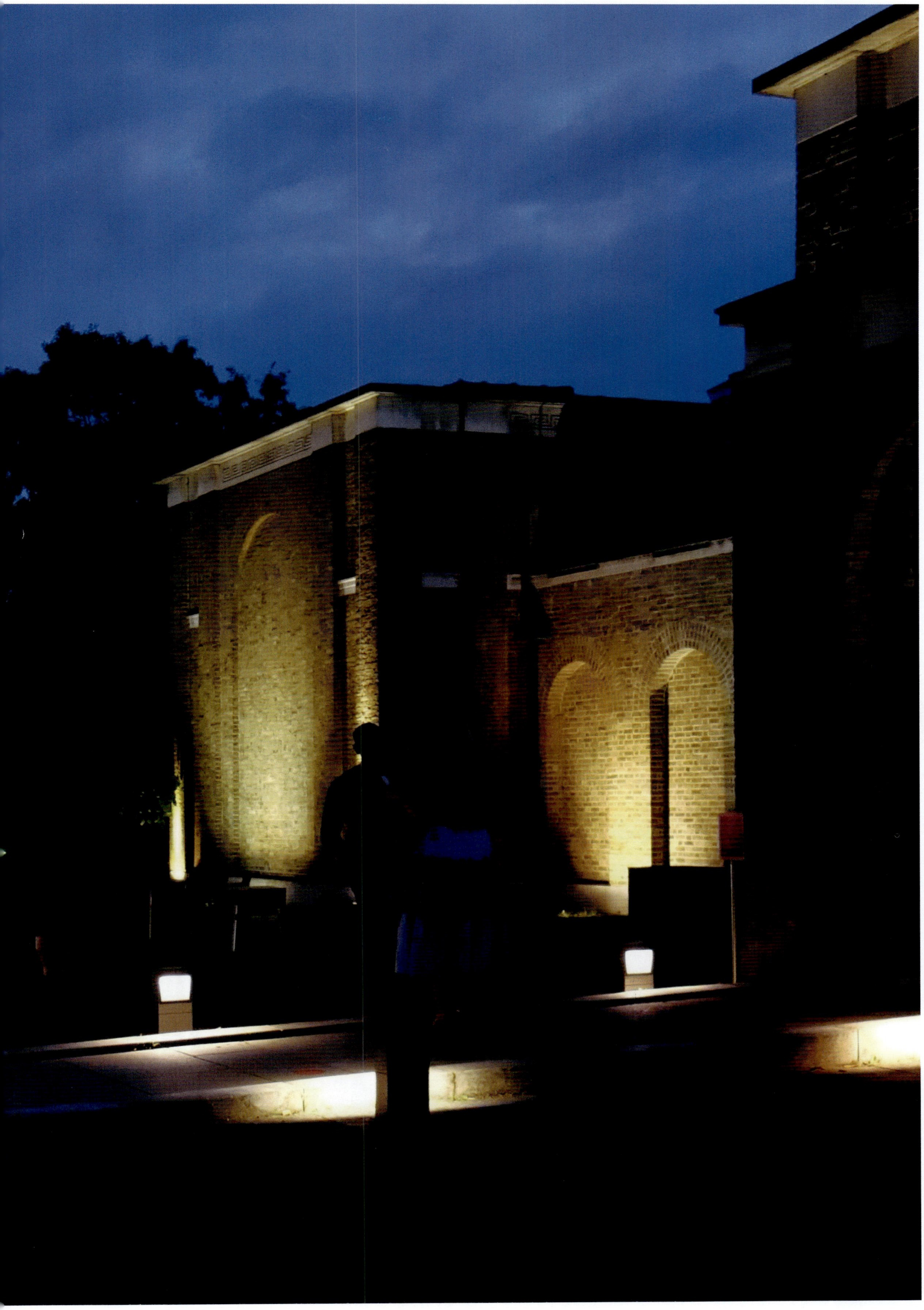

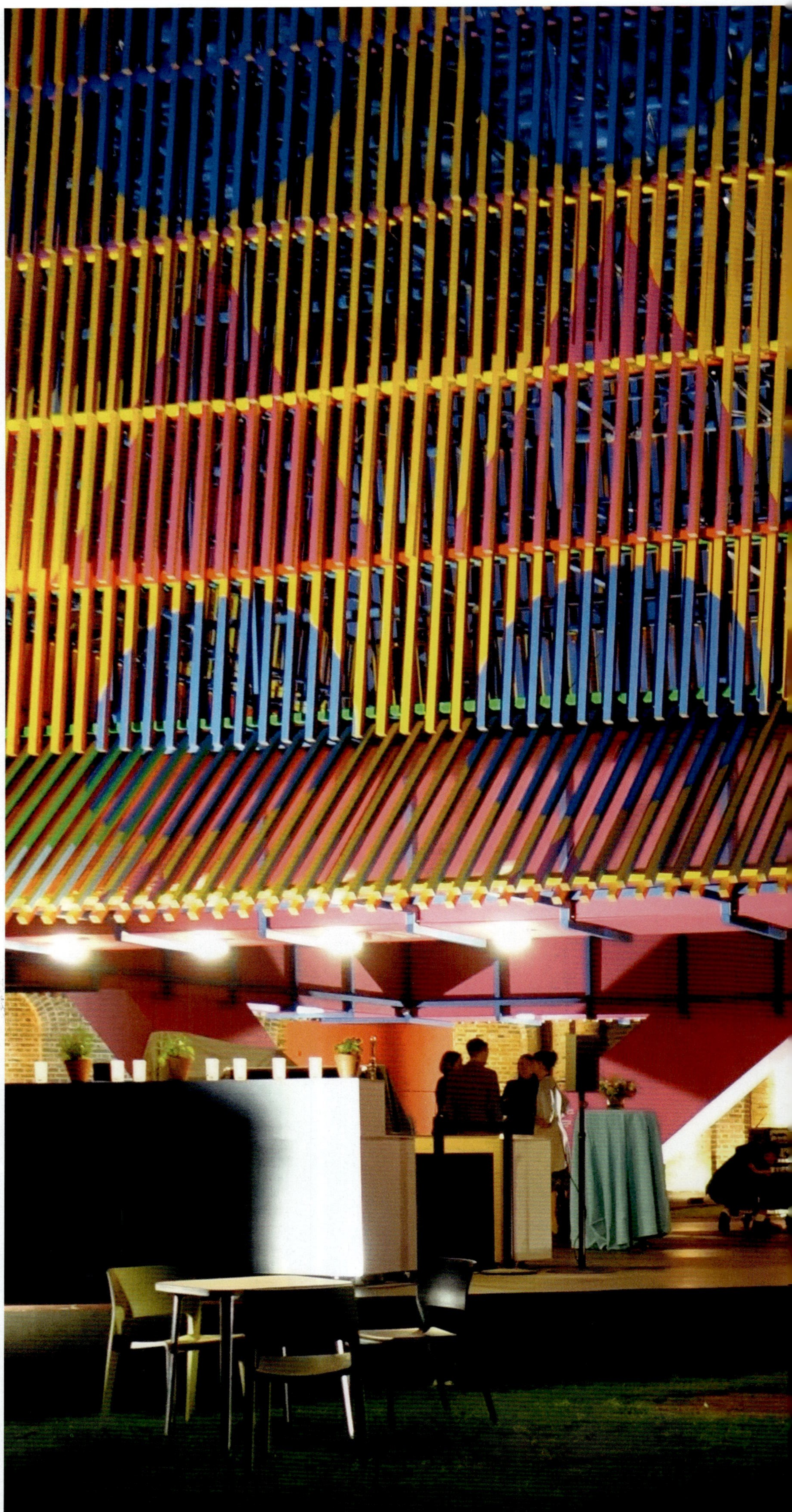

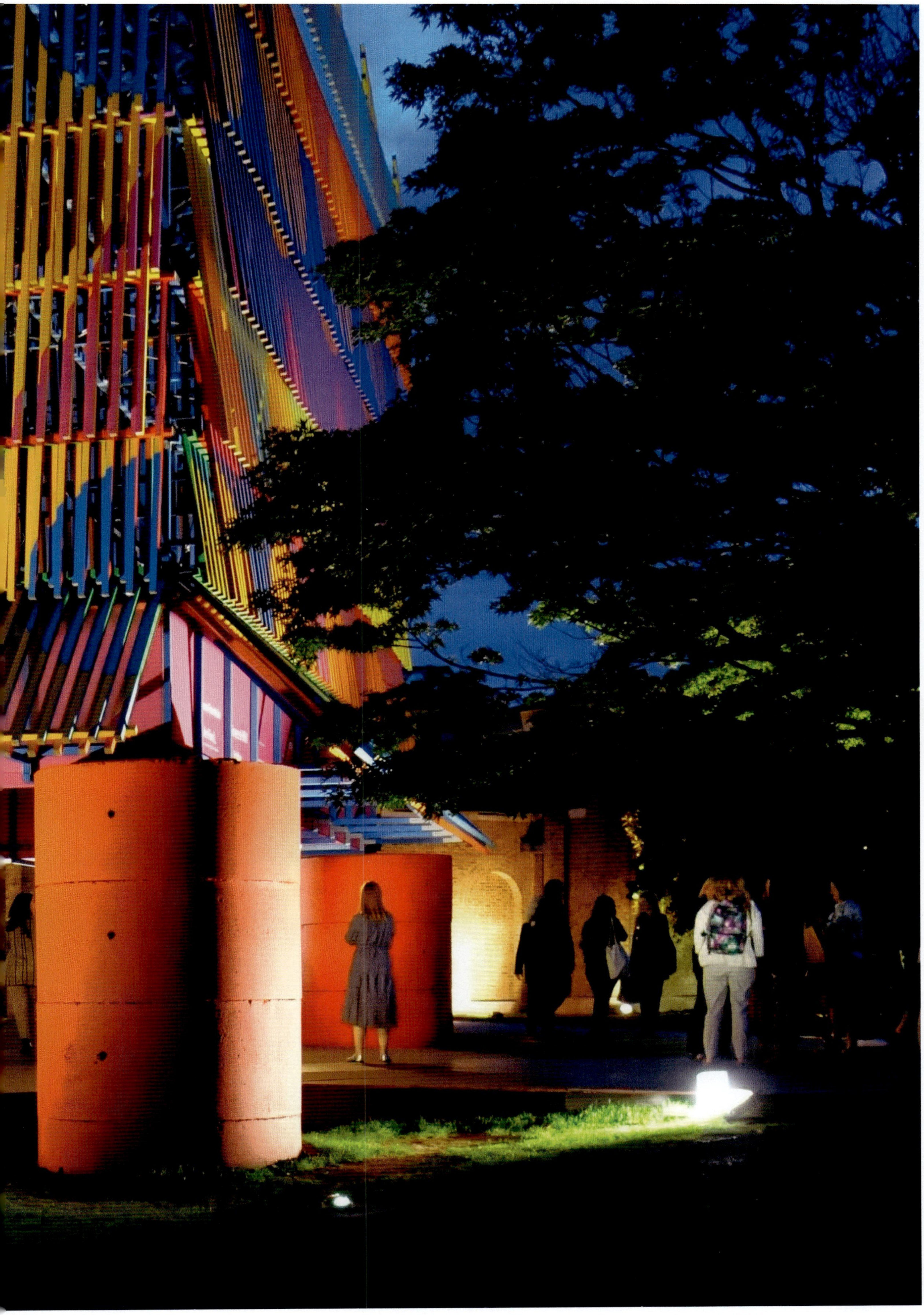

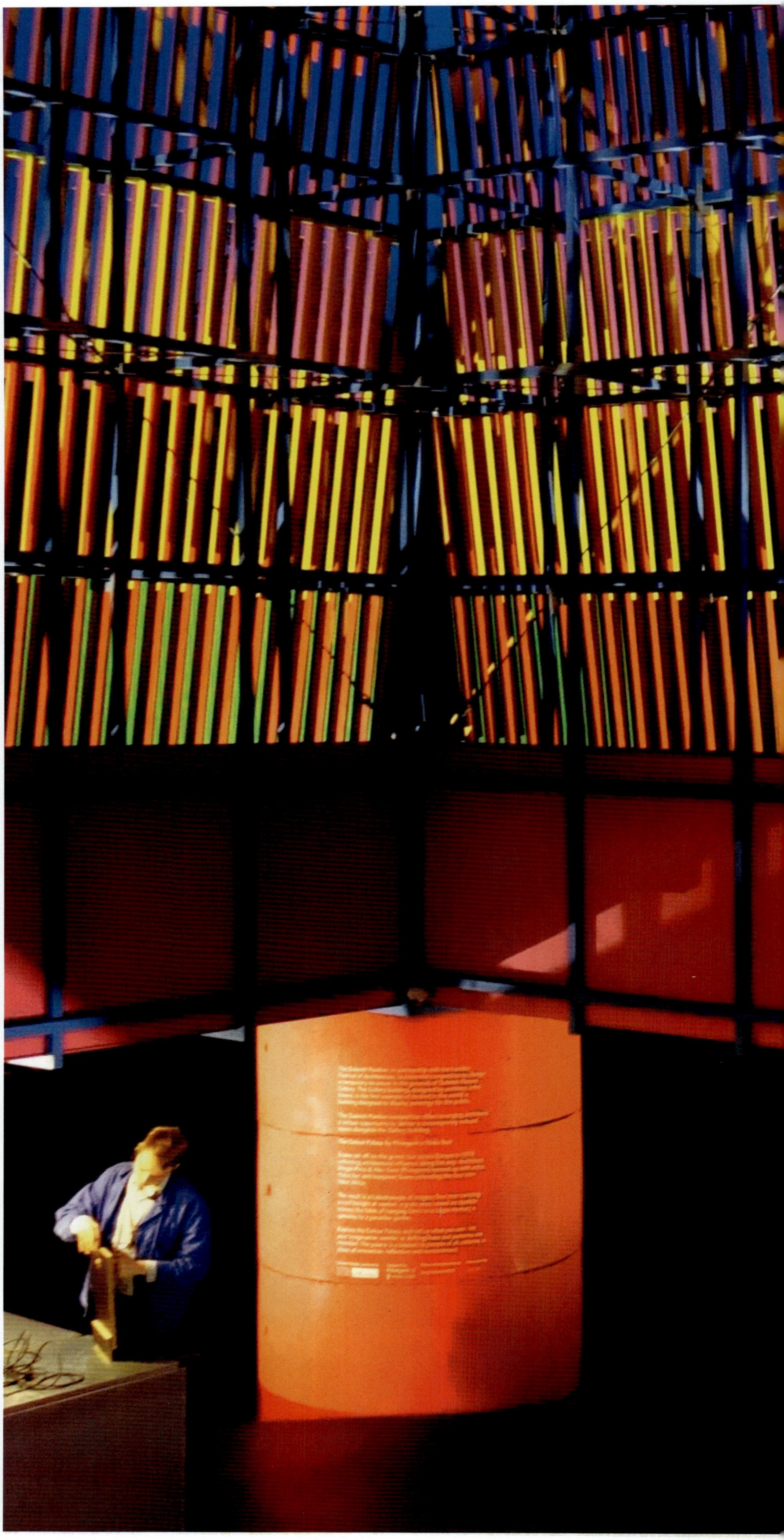

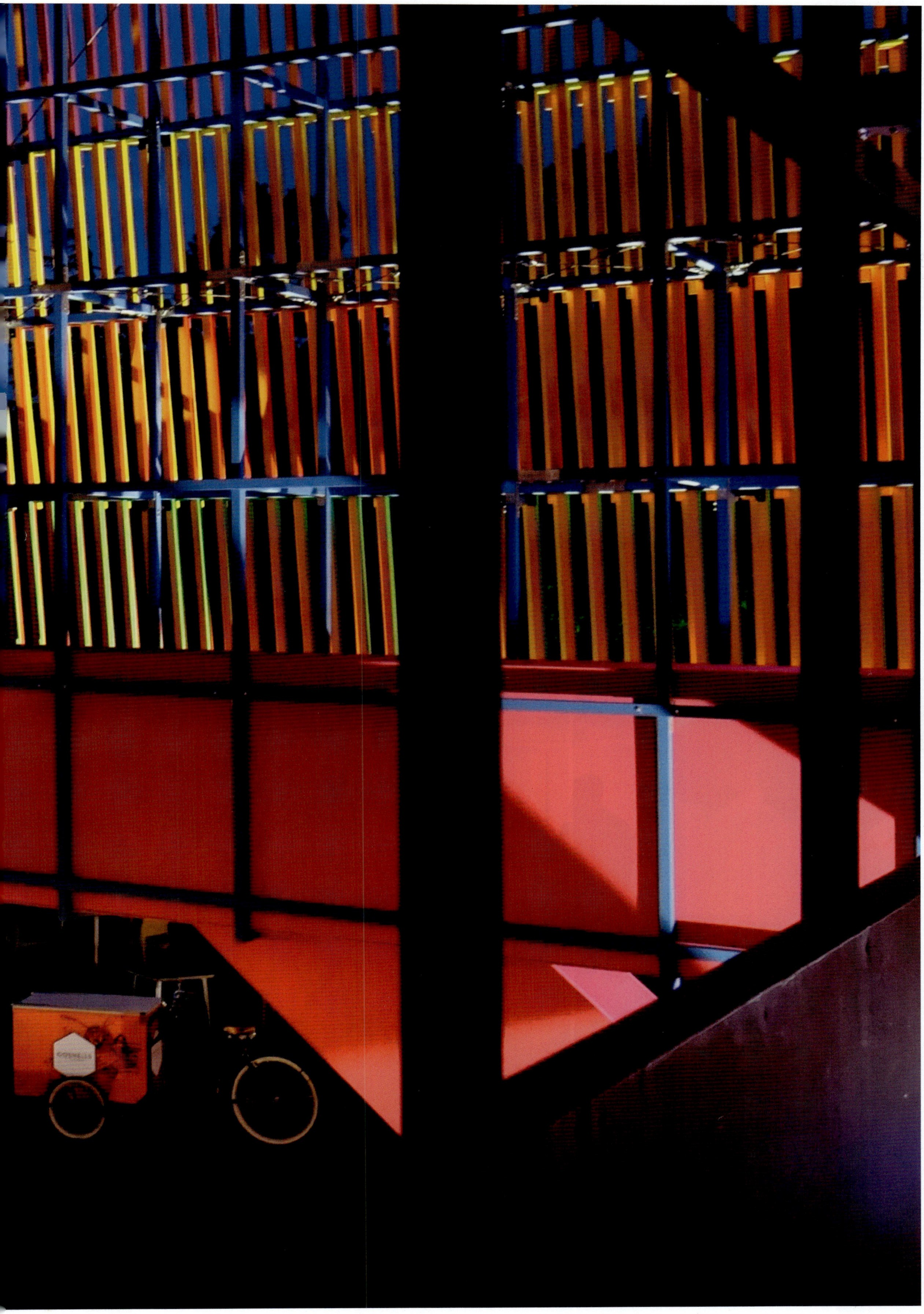

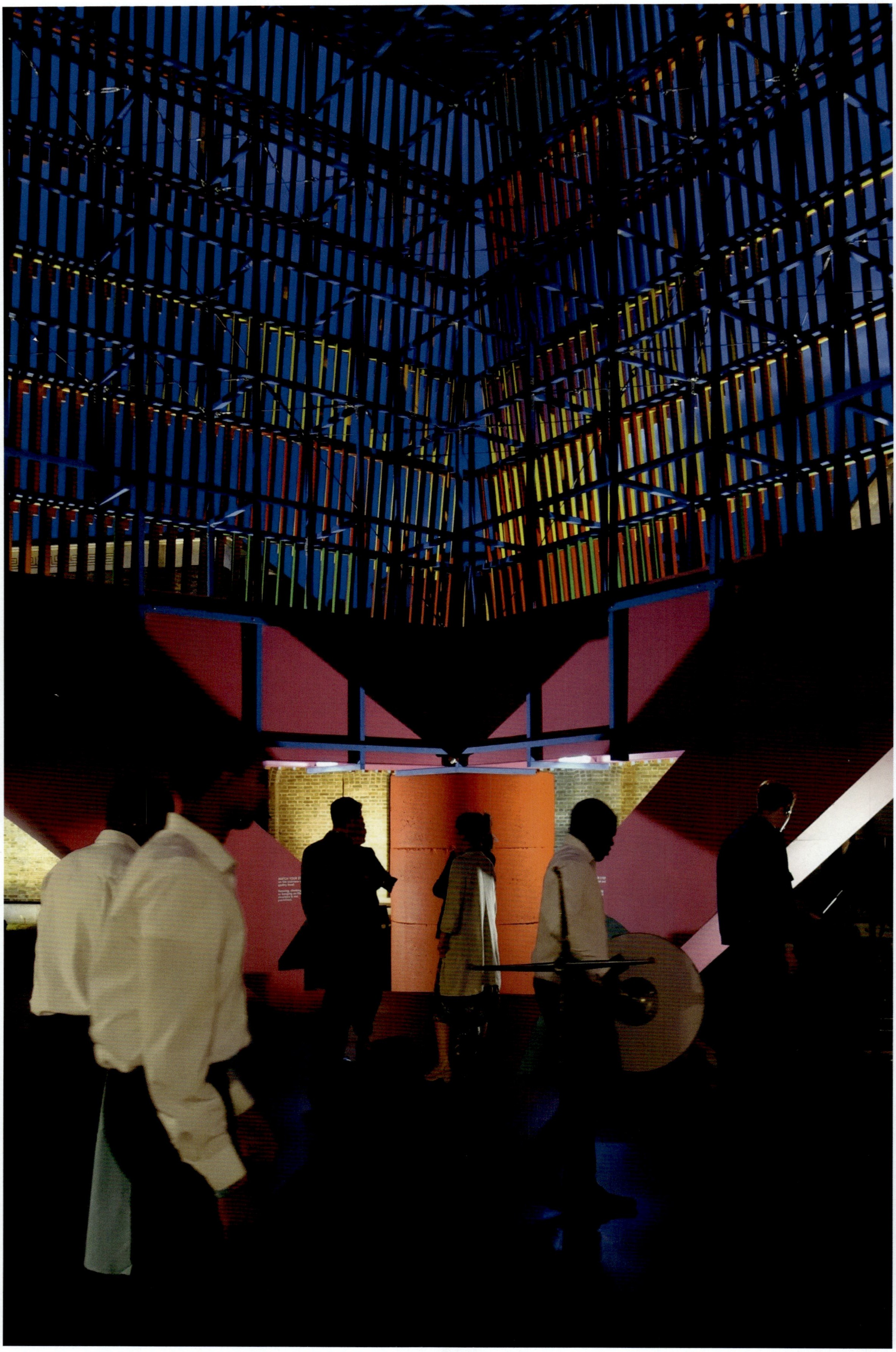

Job Floris
Only but Colour

Here is the proof. The condition of the temporary structure is a treat for architects. Whereas most of the time we architects are involved in extensive, serious, and lengthy building processes, the brief life of a pavilion offers us the thrill of spontaneity. We should approach this type of structure as a place of real-life experiment, an extension of our laboratory, a fertile testing ground. Besides the condition of temporariness creates a window of opportunity for extra direct and bold behaviour: for risks, exaggeration, and daringness. This temporary condition feels enticing and challenging, and it is this cocktail that we encounter in the design of this edition of the Dulwich Pavilion, the 'Colour Palace'.

      While observing this structure, various reflections come to mind. The first is a particular work by the American artist Lawrence Weiner. 'Many Colored Objects Placed Side by Side to Form a Row of Many Colored Objects'[1]. It is a beautiful piece made in text only, executed in dry black capitals, in which Weiner describes the world from the perspective of colour, implying: everything is only but colour. The succinct directness and simplicity of these words coincide with the conceptual basis of the 'Colour Palace' in which colour is the main carrier of meaning. All the rest is secondary. While Weiner embraces the minimal, here the architect and artist have sought a saturated maximum. While the pavilion structure has an effective sobriety, the daring application of colour builds up another narrative. Together, they manage to loosely oscillate between the essential and the added, seeming to effortlessly avoid becoming one-dimensional or

1 'Many Colored Objects Placed Side By Side'. By Lawrence Wiener 1979. From the collection of Annick and Anton Herbert, Ghent, Belgium.

dogmatic. The world of Weiner also comes to mind since this structure is the result of a collaboration between architect and artist. History knows many examples of such challenging collaborations, and too often either the architect or the artist loses some dignity. Here, however, both voices meld remarkably into one convincing tone.

As well as being joyful and direct, the 'Colour Palace' connects to several ancient themes. This is a rare quality, to give birth to a new design which oscillates simultaneously between the past and the present. A connection to the past is made by the typology of the building. It is a folly, historically an object without an explicit function other than a carrier of architectural articulation. The articulation of colour was historically an intrinsic tool of architects as much as of artists. Rich polychromy was used by the Greeks and Romans for animating ceramics, sculptures, and important civic buildings such as temples. In time these colours faded completely and the presence of the far more neutral white base of these classical structures became embedded in collective conscience. For centuries the colour was forgotten and it was gradually assumed that the white, uncovered material was the original intention of the architects. It was the French architect Jacques Ignace Hittorff who shocked the world in the nineteenth century by rediscovering the abundant use of applied colour in classical architecture. Influenced by Hittorff, the German architect Gottfried Semper continued the rehabilitation of colour for architects. In his publication 'The Four Elements of Architecture'[2], polychromy became a solid and elemental topic in his thinking alongside his tectonic theories: about the wall and its cladding, and the idea of dressing. Specifically, Semper embraced the idea of using polychromy to emphasise form over construction: detaching form and materials from each other by making the idea more important than the materials themselves – an idea which proved to be influential for many subsequent generations. It is exactly in this line of thinking that the 'Colour Palace' registers. It resists our collective amnesia by expressing a strong notion of the rich tradition of polychromy. Today the engagement of the majority of architects

[2] 'The Four Elements of Architecture and Other Writings', Gottfrie Semper. Cambridge University Press 2011. Harry Francis Mallgrave, Wolfgang Herrmann.

with colour is a fragile one. For various reasons, the topic of colour adds yet another complexity to the immense mountain of complexities in the process of conceiving, designing and realising a building. For a while, architects retreated to the safe grounds of denial by opting for the honest, original colour of materials, completely satisfied with an illusion of choice. For others, colour stands for a visit to Arcadia resulting in an overdone celebration of colour. Alternatively, colour is used in an operational way: to make corrections, by emphasising parts that might not have worked out well by being too subtle – colour as a cheap saviour. Luckily, other intelligent architects addressed this question – a proper reflection on how to deal with colour in architecture – a while before us. The law of the Viennese architect Adolf Loos on cladding appears to be applicable here: 'Wood may be painted in any colour except one – the colour of wood.'[3] The pavilion seems to suggest this simple and direct treatment of the relation between material and colour remains ever valid and accurate. Just like in the architecture of Loos, colour is not something that could be omitted from the pavilion. Yet, if we manage to imagine the structure beyond the coloured surface, in accordance with the white temples, no misinterpretation could be possible: this pavilion is to be understood as a piece of clever craftsmanship: the economy of means is palpable.

  In the 'Colour Palace', there are no immediate details revealing its actual size and scale. This calm treatment brings the structure into the World of Objects. Think of the drawings by the Italian architect Aldo Rossi, among others, who places ordinary domestic elements among buildings – and scales parts of buildings into domestic elements, as if they are equal. Indeed, they are equal. Both small and large objects have the ability to be charged with an abundance of intention and gesture, no matter the scale. The specific object-treatment of the coloured structure seems to use the seductive strategies of everyday packaging design – novel forms, brightly coloured and accoutred with the elementary forms of circles, squares, and triangles. More intriguing is the phenomenon of depth created by the shifting

[3] 'The Principle of Cladding,' 'Spoken into the Void: Collected Essays, 1897–1900, Adolf Loos, published for the Graham Foundation for Advanced Studies in the Fine Arts, Chicago, IL, and the Institute for Architecture and Urban Studies, New York, NY, by MIT Press, Oppositions Books.

of colours: the front of each wooden batten is painted with a colour that differs from the sides. This can be understood both as emphasising the depth, also as completely denying depth by emphasising the surface layer of colour, as if it were flat, as if it were coloured Rizla, paper-thin. The reading of lightness is confirmed by the peaks on the roof which make a relation to the roof of Sir Soane's Picture Gallery. Behaving slightly like crenellations, they simultaneously confirm the billboard-like thinness of the facades. This provocative simplicity adds a light tone of voice, and forms a welcome counterpoint to the monumental form of the structure.

      This idiosyncratic pavilion brings to mind ideas of eclecticism, mannerism, ornamentation, and irony – all of which allude to the topic of postmodernism in architecture. This might be a simplification, as the object is obviously informed by a larger realm of things. Yet, the traces are undeniably there. Although revivals of postmodernity have been in the air for at least a decade, what we have here is different. This traces back to the moment where many of us departed from the abundance of postmodernism. Perhaps, in search of calm essentialism, we were rejecting it for the wrong reasons, something we are now able to admit. With more experience we now appreciate its ingenuity, recognise the references, the historic precedents, and their translation in a light and joyful way. With this new insight, we have aimed for continuity by extracting the good lessons of postmodernism and enhancing them with other schools of architectural thinking. For example, recent attempts to activate a layer of tactility and material specificity, which were so often absent in the early works of postmodernism. By choosing a few ingredients instead of a multitude. By being less literal and more resonant. And by avoiding dead end – and arrogant cynicism, while enjoying irony. None of this is easy: misunderstandings are common as we figure out the rules of the playing field, and whether to break them. Contemporary discourse about postmodern architecture is often simplistic, treating it altogether as a low-res container, whilst in reality it covers a rich multitude of perspectives. Clearly these matters have been carefully considered and informed the element of risk in the design of the 'Colour Palace'. With its lite-appearance and profound intentions, it offers a moment of provocation and reflection in the on-going discourse.

Sumayya Vally
Footnotes to a Palace

Consider this text a holding place – holding shifting habitats, evolving legacies, residues and futures of places and publics.

01 51.4433° N, 0.0676° W

02 967. Edgar the Peaceful granted Dilwihs to a thane.

03 Dilwihs, Dylways, Dullag – from two Old English words, Dill, a white flower, and wihs, meaning a damp meadow: 'the meadow where dill grows'

04 Hall Place, established thirteenth century, later moated with a barn, stables, outhouses, yards and 30 acres of rich pasture, gardens and orchard.

05 1333. A population of 100.

Dulwich, historically 'more exclusive'

06 1619. The College of God's Gift founded by the actor Edward Alleyn. Also includes almshouses and a school for underprivileged boys.

07 1719–31. Francis Lynn of Hall Place, Dulwich, Secretary of The Royal Africa Trading Company.

08 1778. John Soane architect departs for Rome, the first leg of his Grand Tour of Europe.

09 1790. King Stanislaus Augustus of Poland appoints art dealers Noël Desenfans and Sir Francis Bourgeois to assemble a Royal Collection.

10 They devote the next five years to this task, Acquiring Italian, Spanish, French, Flemish, and Dutch works of art, mainly of the seventeenth and eighteenth century.

11 1795. Poland is partitioned by its neighbours, leading to its complete disappearance as an independent state. The King is forced to abdicate, leaving the dealers with a 'Royal' collection on their hands.

12 1811. Dulwich Picture Gallery – England's first purpose-built public art gallery – is founded by the terms of Sir Francis Bourgeois' will.

13 1814. Soane builds the picture gallery and the founder's mausoleum. Severe neo-Greek style, yellow brick with stone dressings.

14 1817. The gallery opens to the public. Frequented by many cultural figures over the next hundred years, including John Constable, J.M.W. Turner, and later Vincent van Gogh.

15 Dulwich gallery gardens: numerous trees of interest;

16 *Juglans regia*, the Persian walnut, English walnut, Carpathian walnut, Madeira walnut, or especially in Great Britain, common walnut, is an Old World walnut tree species native to the region stretching from the Balkans, eastward to the Himalayas and southwest China.

17 Buxus – a genus of about 70 species in the family *Buxaceae*. Common names include box or boxwood. Native to Africa, Madagascar, northernmost South America, Central America, Mexico, and the Caribbean, western and southern Europe, southwest, southern, and eastern Asia, with the majority of species being tropical or subtropical.

The Age of Imperialism, territories are bound.

18 1833. The Slavery Abolition Act.

19 1881. The 'Scramble for Africa' begins. 90% of African continent under European control by 1914.

20 A list of losses of independence: Egypt to the UK, Merina to France, Bechuanaland to the UK, Ijebu to the UK, Oubangui-Chari to France, Rwanda to Germany, Dahomey to France, Bunyoro to the UK, Kingdom of Benin to the UK, Burundi to Germany, Ashanti Confederacy to the UK, Swaziland to the UK, Fulani Empire to France and the UK, Libya to Italy, Morocco to France.

21 1884. United Kingdom establishes the Oil River Protectorate in Nigeria. An economic system designed to profit from African labour: the British pound sterling – which could be demanded through taxation, paid to cooperative natives, and levied as a fine.

22 Nigeria: total area of 98 million hectares, of which 71 million hectares can be cultivated: oil, cocoa, groundnut, soy, cotton, fish, palm oil, rubber.

Active leftovers, quiet histories, silent sovereignties, gradated empires, 'new' categorisations and carceral atlases of colony.

23 1893 Dulwich. 1894 Brixton. The first sightings of parakeets in the UK, a non-migratory species of bird, native to Africa and the Indian subcontinent.

24 Also reported to have escaped from the film set of 'The African Queen', Ealing Studios. Others are released by Jimi Hendrix in Carnaby Street. Now reported to number 30,000 in Britain.

25 1901. The Horniman Museum – founded upon the wealth of the tea trade – opens a short walk from Dulwich Picture Gallery.

26 Large 'African' collection including religious and ritual artefacts, weapons and jewellery taken by British troops in an invasion of the Kingdom of Benin. Also known for its collection of taxidermy.

27 1917. World War I. German East African Campaign. Battles between native African soldiers under the command of their respective colonial powers.

28 1939–45. World War II. Britain enlists 3 million soldiers from colonial territories.

29 1960s. A community of Nigerians first settle in neighbouring Peckham. Now sometimes known as Little Lagos, it is part of a community of some 100,000 Nigerian-born Londoners.

30 1971. Fela Kuti records his second album, 'Fela's London Scene', at Abbey Road Studios with Tony Allen and Ginger Baker on drums, having previously graduated from Trinity College of Music.

31 1990. Margaret Thatcher leaves Downing Street and moves into Hambledon Place, a gated development in Dulwich.

32 2011 Census. Southwark. 54.3% White, 26.8% Black, 9.5% Asian, 6.2% Mixed, 0.8% Arab, 2.4% Other.

The contested effectiveness of migration policy.

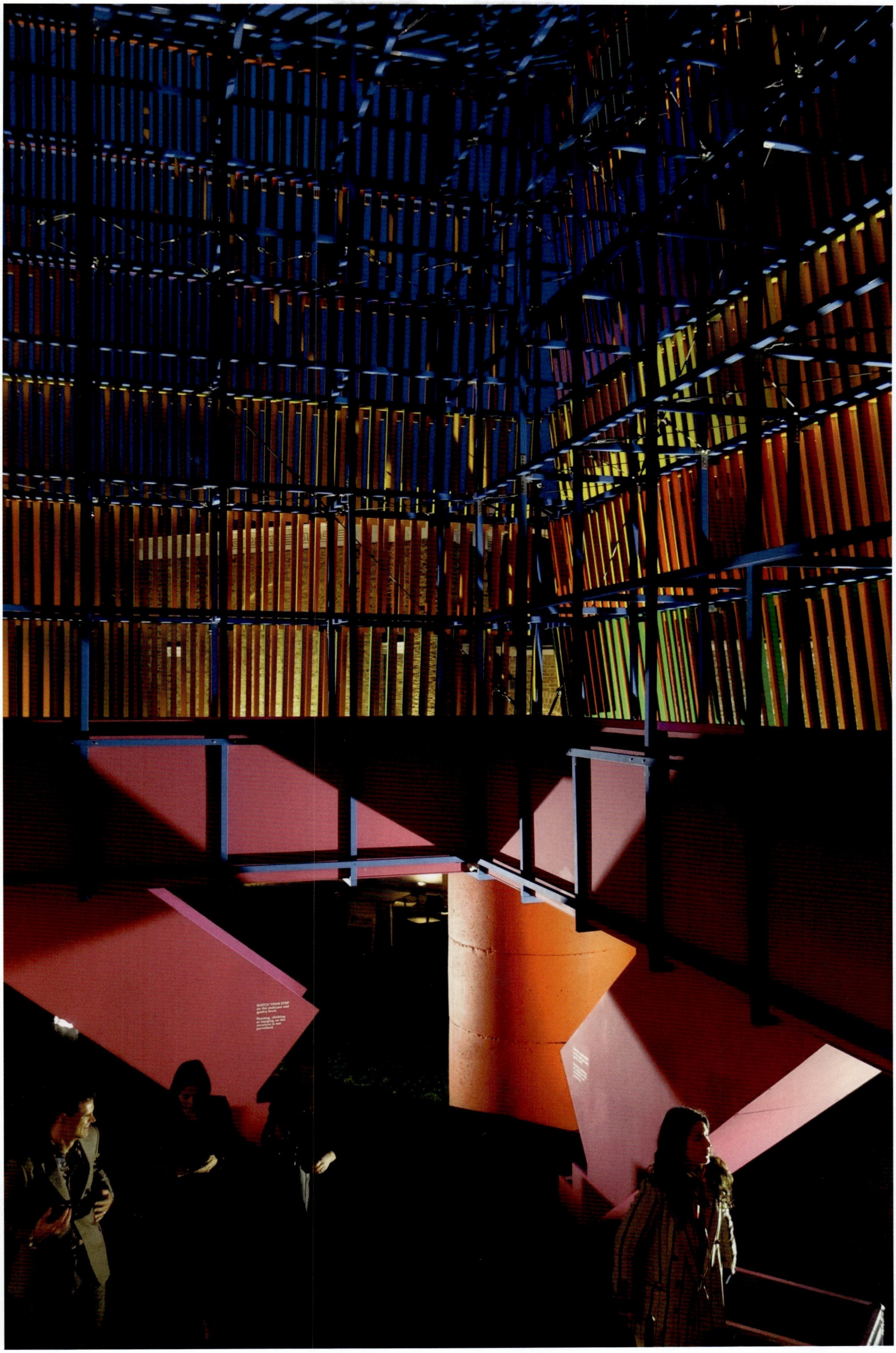

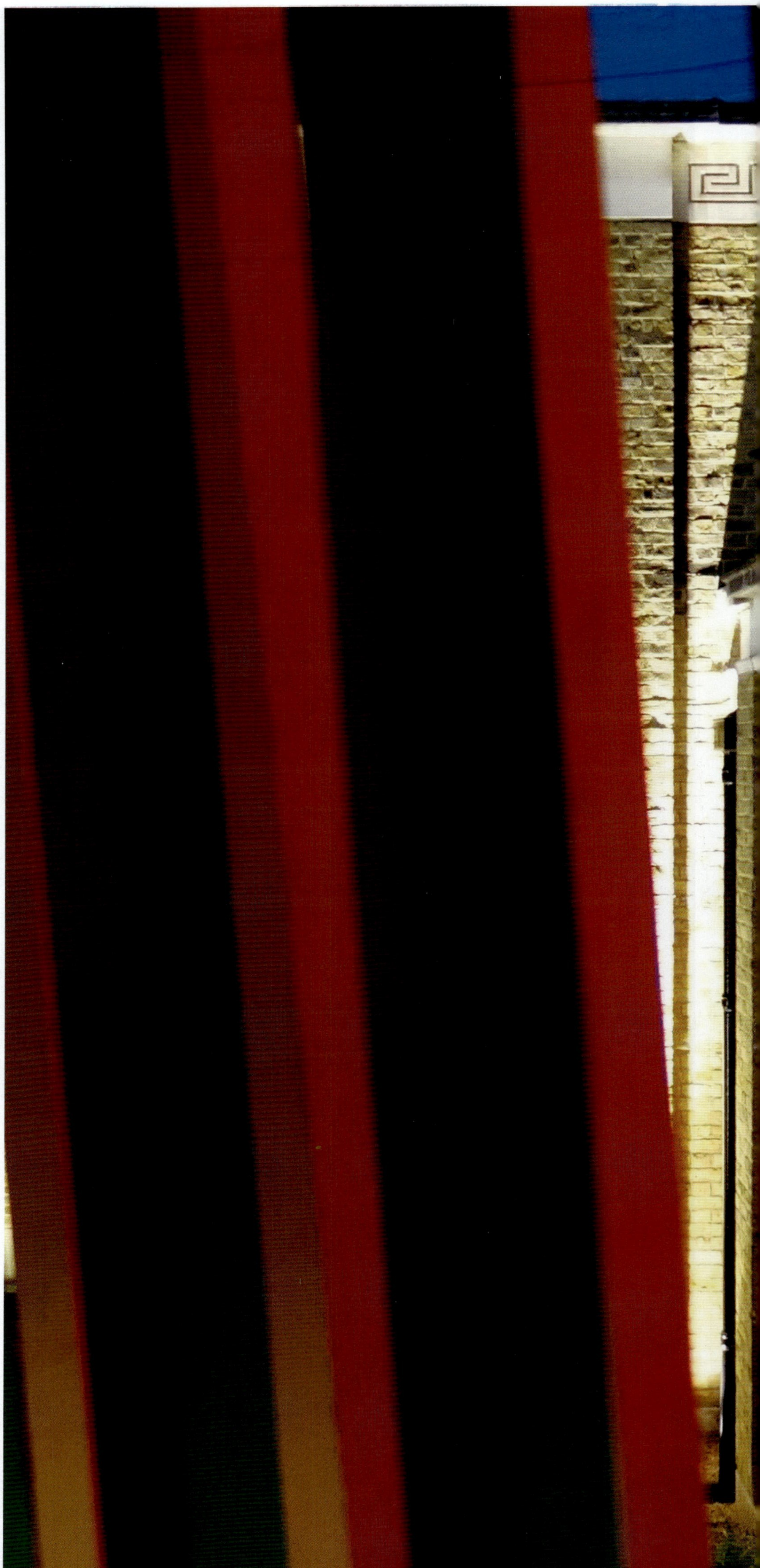

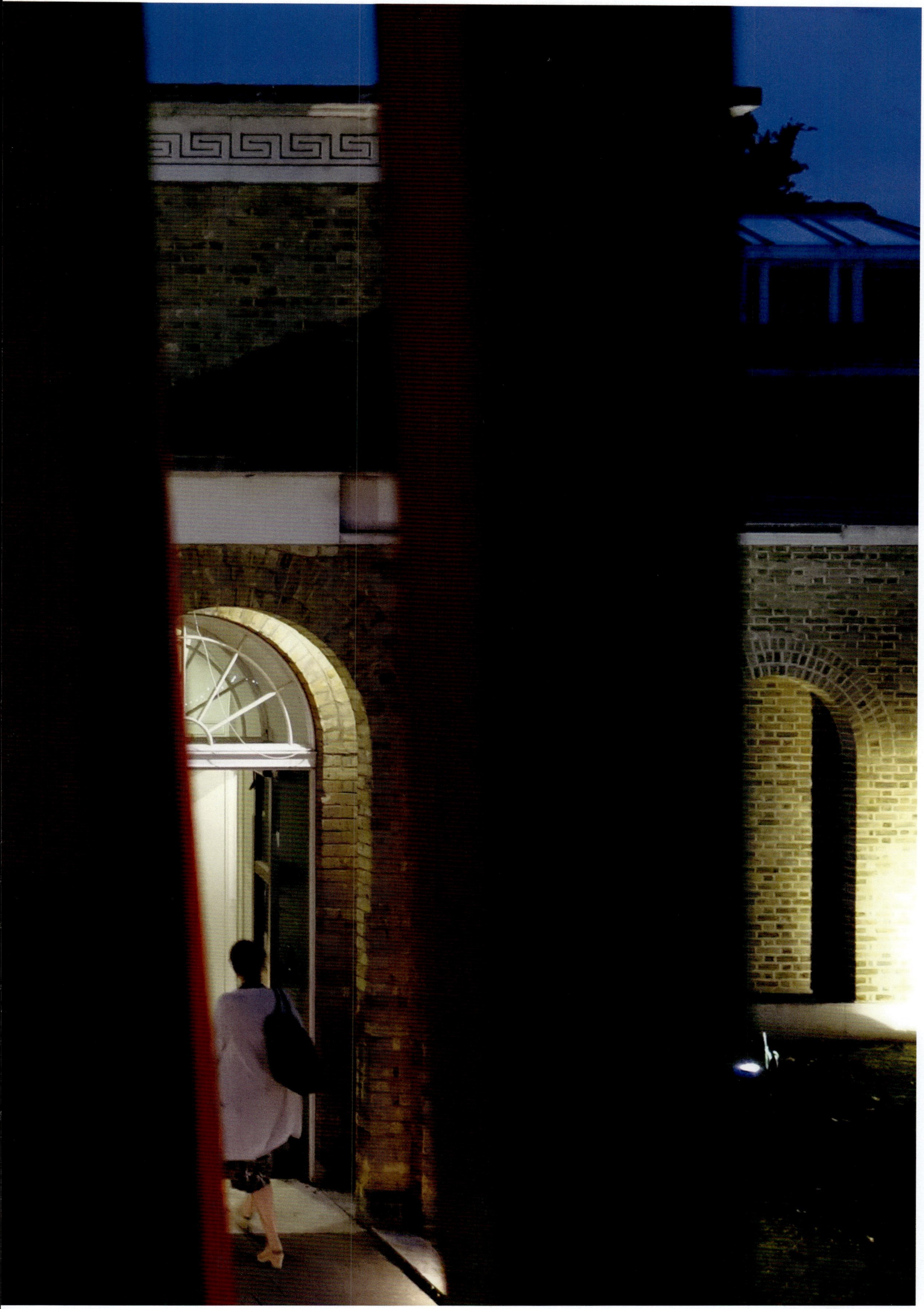

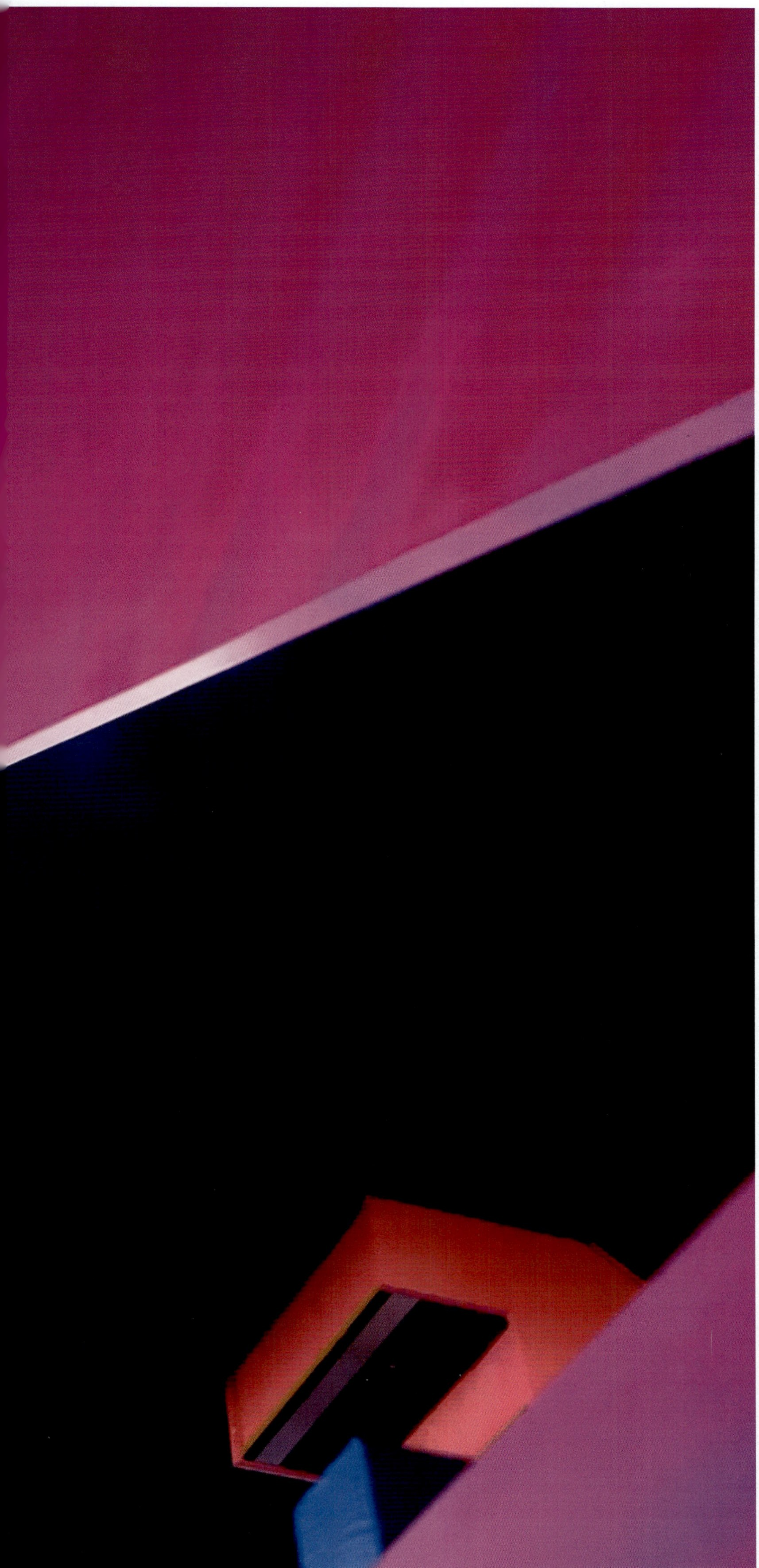

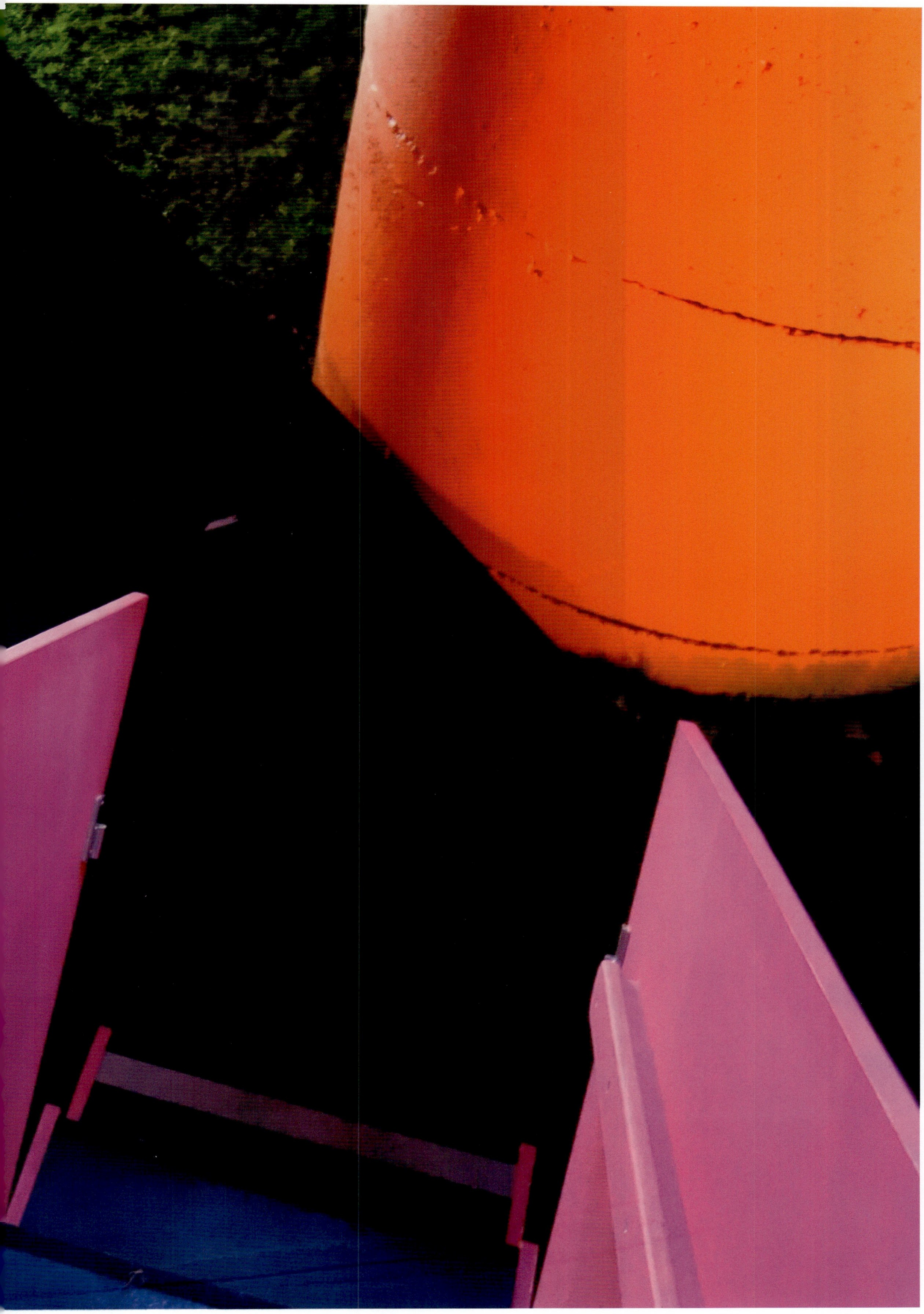

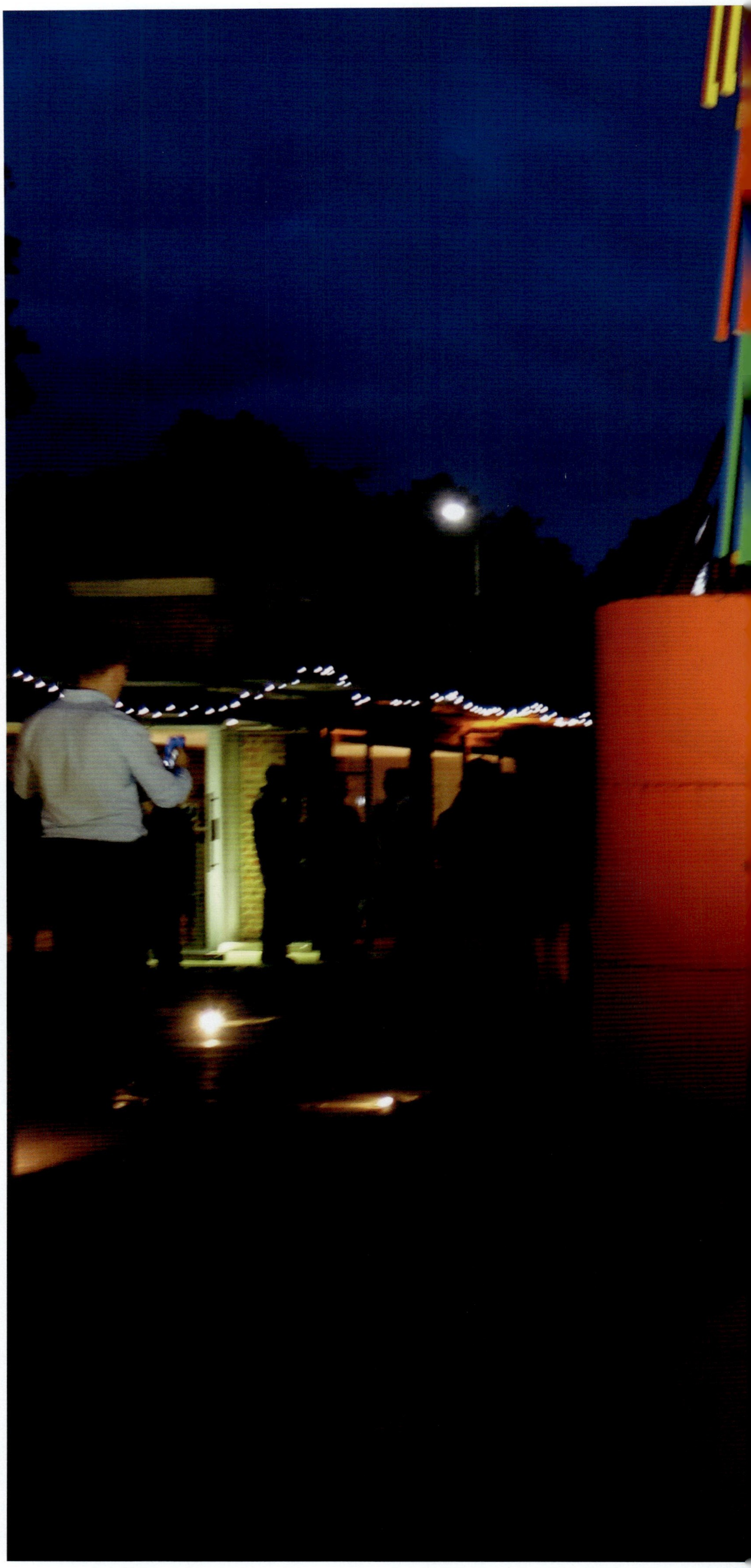

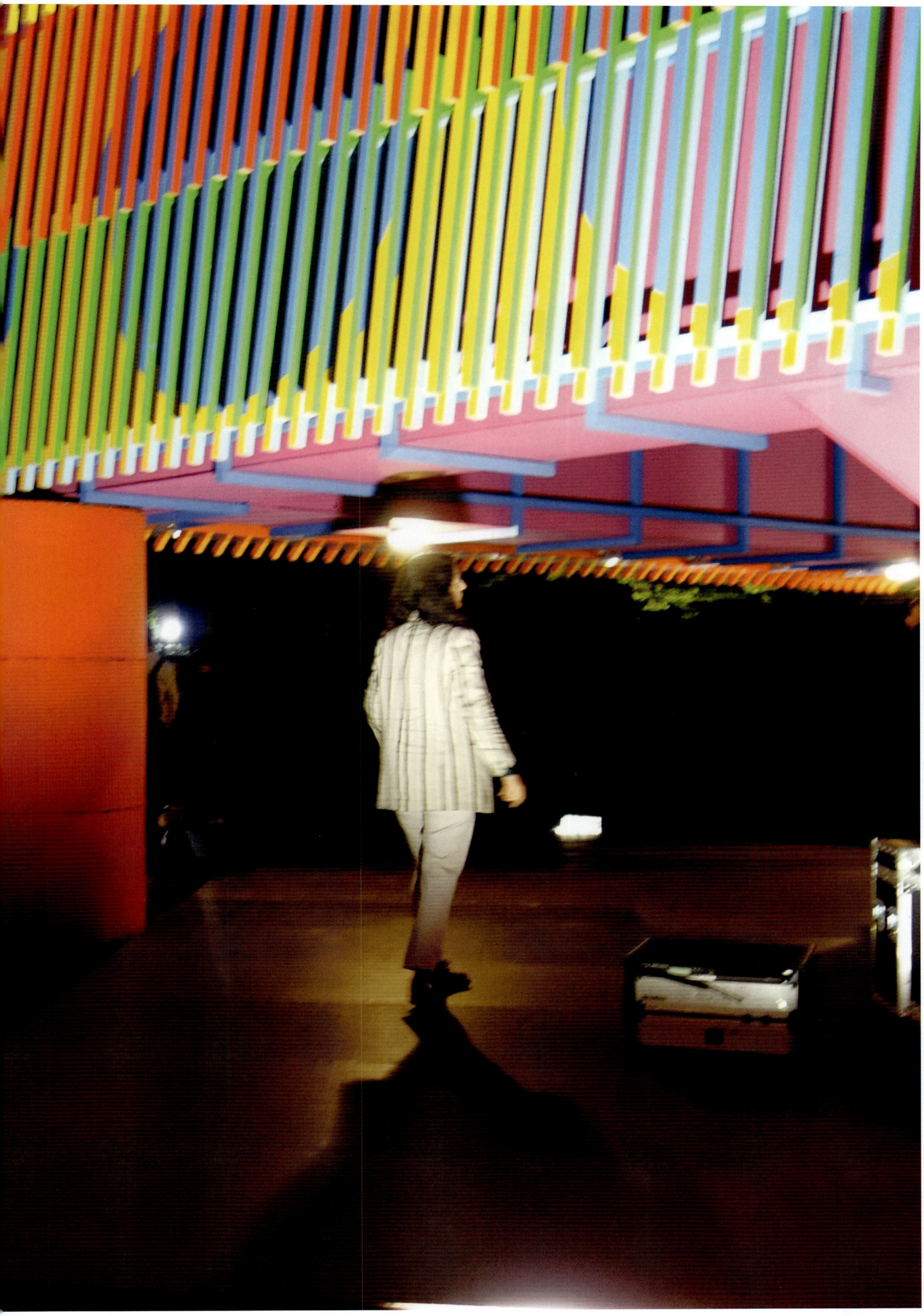

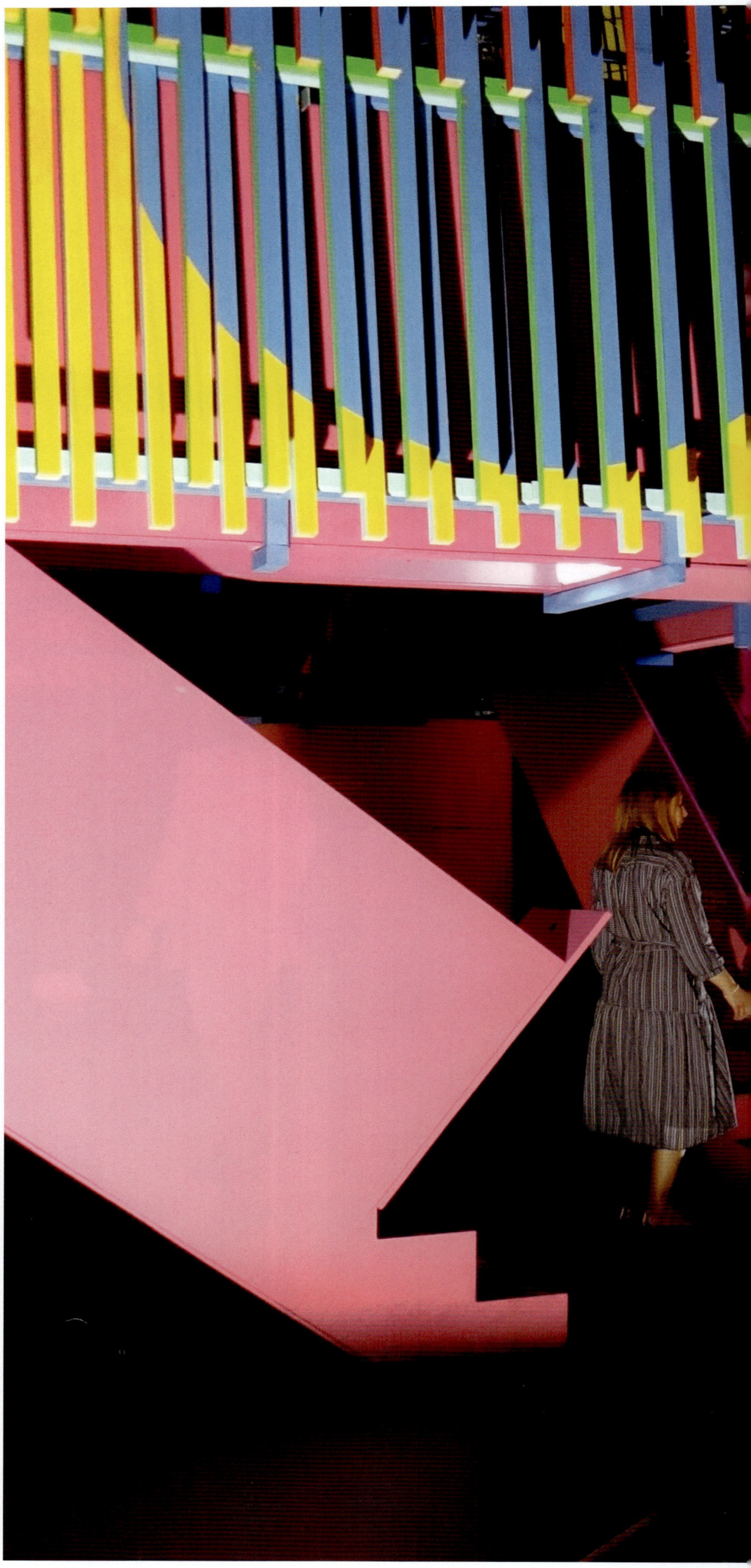